Secrets of Sheets

Secrets of Sheets

Pamela L. Laskin

Plain View Press
P. O. 42255
Austin, TX 78704

plainviewpress.net
sb@plainviewpress.net
1-512-441-2452

Copyright: Pamela L. Laskin 2009. All rights reserved.
ISBN: 978-0-911051-66-7
Library of Congress Number: 2009920241

Cover art by Kirsi Tuomanen Hill

Acknowledgments

Acknowledgment is made to the following publications in which these poems first appeared:

"Heart of Nothing," "Times Square" ... *Array*
"Dry Cleaners" ... *bestpoem 2008*
"The Shomer" ... *Garfield Anthology*
"One, One Shoe" ... *Global City Review 18*
"Like Magic" ... *Out of Line*
"Yom Kippur" ... *Poetica*
"Crossing Borders," "Losses" ... *Poetry in Performance*, 1999, 2002
"The Jungle," "The Whale" ... *Promethean*
"Metaphor" ... *Steam Ticket*

To Ira—with you there are no secrets

Table of Contents

I. Yours   13

Cremation	15
One	16
The Jungle	17
The Whale	18
Refuse	19
Adolescence	20
Homeless, Summer, 1999	21
Stolen Body	22
Away: A Found Poem from the NYT	23
Welfare Reform	24
Welfare: A Child's Voice	25
Like Magic	26
Always Hungry	27
Chicken Little	28
This Christmas....	29
The Shomer	30
Tsunami	31
T.W.A. Crash	32
The Bomber	33
My Baby	34
The Heart of Nothing	35
Garden of Birth/Absence of Earth	36
Darfur	37
Losses: The War in Kosovo	38
Crossing Borders	39
Eleanora's Collage	40
With Poems	41
Other People's Laundry	42

II. Mine   45

The Laundress	47
Vacation	48
One Shoe	49
Season of Sorrow	50
Amsterdam	51
Grades	53

Signals	54
Yom Kippur	55
The Tapestry	56
A Motherless Traveler	57
Longing	58
The Journal	59
Times Square, Christmas, 1960	60
The Cape	61
Death of an I.U.D.	62
Shroud Lifted	64
In Harbor	65
Sunset	66
Navigations	67
The Man	68
Cruise Liner	69
Clean Laundry	70
Metaphor	71
Departure	73
Dry Cleaners	74
About the Author	77

I. Yours

Cremation

All
that's in our waste
is hidden.
We dispose
our love letters, dirty diapers,
shredded tissues
often tear-saturated
and sometimes
filled with blood,
so that no trace
of the self
is in the house
other than the furniture, appliances, bedding
and the secrets of the sheets.

One

It's only
one gene
that makes my toddler talk
while the child
in the stroller
mutters gibberish
to the wind;

one stray sperm
that splits
instead of somersaults
that gave me
a schizophrenic mother
while you
were fed on fortune's food,

food
never again eaten
for the one step taken
when the Nazis invaded
the secret hiding space,

one secret discovered
one fairly unremarkable moment,

can make a life
many lives
disappear
quicker than a breath
the swish of blood
the beat of a heart,

one kiss
that she gets
instead of me.

The Jungle

Looking at you—
stomach ballooning over pants
teeth cracked and yellow
wearing a wardrobe of dirt
under your nails
where it lingered
like rotten earth;

made me enter
the HEART OF DARKNESS
shaded shadows of your hunched-over form,
words of wonder
churning in dire, dark waters.

I read you, as such
and never left the jungle.

The Whale

Smelling like a sewer
you hobbled
into the center
like a whale on wheels,
one with dirty fins
and bulging blubber;
one whose low, piercing moan
could be heard
in miles
of wet tears of water;

but you didn't cry when you spoke these stories
you just said them
then swam away.

Refuse

There
in the groins
of the subway tracks-
the handkerchief
choked with semen
you've discarded.

The stain remains
even when a stranger
washes it,
sends it to the cleaners,

dump your dirt
but you can't hide,
the train still rumbles
littered by your lies.

Adolescence

Strange bird
ready
to soar in the sky;

(perched
in position
wings uplifted
front foot forward);

and for a moment
you reach the moon like magic,

stay in the air
lifted at last
as high as you can fly,

but then you tumble
poor pigeon,
why does the ground seem better?

Homeless, Summer, 1999

Does it matter
that this bird
has nowhere to go?

Its wounded wing
has stopped it
from flying.

And now
on the beach
in summer
it staggers
in between towels
and overgrown radios;

it circles the sand
frantic with hunger

having lost
his friends
and youth,
his place
in the universe.

Stolen Body

"The woman stole my card," she shouts;
"the woman stole my watch," she screams
and when no one listens,
"the woman stole my body."

A nurse
gives her a wink,
moves
rushes past the body
draped in schmatas;

what is left
is seventy years
of bones.

Yes, she is crying
no, there is nothing
anyone can do,
but wink, move on
pretend
she's just another lunatic
let loose from the asylum.

Away: A Found Poem from the NYT

She was learning disabled
so I shot her
through the heart,
seven years
and dumb as a door-nail.

I didn't want her to die,
I just wanted to stop
being her mother—
the soccer season was coming up
and a dance recital
where all she could talk about
was the blue ruffles;

not math
not science
not reading

just blue ruffles
as large as dreams
that could take her
far, far away.

Welfare Reform

"Vey es mir,"
I've lived
within this casket of bones
for ninety-six years
in one room
with a hot plate
and running water;
it was better in Russia.

But my brother-in-law
God bless his soul;
he's been dead
for thirty years;
he never told
me
to become a citizen.

"Vey es mir,"
my next-door neighbor, Harry
a youngster at eighty-five
and blind,
told me the government has no allowance
for us anymore.

Time to park the casket
on the street.

Welfare: A Child's Voice

Papa got da' blues
from hanging out in jail;

Mama got da' runs
and boy is mama frail;

Tommy got a toothache
with no medicine to take;

and me, I got this hunger
and this hunger
ain't no fake.

Like Magic

Describe
the architecture of bones
on this boy's body—
ribs
as brittle as twigs
barely hold together
flesh;

now
the flesh will disappear
like magic,
since the check will disappear
like magic.

Always Hungry

Oh, child
here's your punishment
for being poor—
nothing to eat
no check
to carry mama through the month;

forget about Christmas,
a new coat for winter;
last year you were so cold
your ribs were icicles.
So what?

Who asked to be born
to a crack-head parent
who now, drug-free
wants a job
for more than
five dollars an hour.

Not the government's problem!
there are more children than puppies
and they're always hungry.

Chicken Little

    9/11

"Chicken Little,
Chicken Little
the sky is falling;"

no child's play
no trampoline
to catch the debris;

no ground
to bury the sorrow
too much weight—

the sorrow
the sky
the little chicken

who never imagined
a fairy-tale
turned real, turned ugly.

This Christmas....

1.
the wrapping
is deceptive;

no gift
but guns, garbage
graffiti of bodies;

my father
beneath it all,

and he thought
the box
could protect him.

11.
Underneath the tree~
abundance.
Beneath the heart—
absence.

The Shomer

    A found poem from the NYT

Every Friday
they descend
on the dungeons of despair—
Ground Zero
the cemetery
with body parts, not bodies
burning in fire.

When the sun
drops its lopsided
 head in darkness,
several young Sabbath beauties
arrive,
Book of Psalms in hands.

Sitting shmira
a task ordinarily given to a man
now performed by women

who sit vigil
over all the arms, legs, broken torsos,
severed heads

because the dead
can't be left alone
from the moment of passing
until burial.

Tsunami

Here
I am autistic
walking through the rummage
of broken bodies
blown away
by reckless waves,
water
that has stolen my words
my comprehension
my desire
to do anything
but bang my head
against the wall,
and bury my language
in the battered bones
of sorrow.

T.W.A. Crash

Two hundred ten bodies
broken past recognition
hide in the water
severed crabs
who might be eaten by sharks
or float, indefinitely
like lost cargo
without a mother ship.

The Bomber

Who
could plant a bomb
walk away
have lunch, take a shower
sleep soundlessly like a kitten;

while hundreds of bodies
ignited alive
fly in the air
before drowning,

many of them children
who won't live
to blow out
their next candle.

My Baby

Was on that plane
blown
to smithereens;

my baby
was sixteen
had saved her baby-sitting money
for this trip to Paris;
I gave her my fifteen hundred dollar
inheritance.

My baby
who bathed her C.P. sister
baby-sat her brother
nursed vigorously
and wanted to see the world;

this child
is dead.
And they can't find
her body.

The Heart of Nothing

It's like drowning
in the sky,
adrift in the dark meat
as fire and waves wash over me,
breaking
piece by piece
into the currents
into the heart
of nothing.

Garden of Birth/Absence of Earth

The sound of fingertips
on her spine
her belly, her lips;

the music
of her heartbeat;
it's louder than the guns

at least
to the mothers
one Israeli, one Palestinian

two women
who once breathed in the garden of birth
now bleed in the absence of earth.

Darfur

There's no laundry here,
you wear
what's on your back,
even that
is burnt and ravaged;
shoes-
in your dreams
ones that will closet
bloody blisters.

Losses: The War in Kosovo

To lose your home
to lose your children;
to carry just the rags on your back
to walk many miles through the mud
and desecrated villages;
to feel the pebbled-ground
torturing your thin-soled feet;
to search the soldier's dark eyes like a crystal ball
and see nothing in his irises
not even
your reflection.

Crossing Borders

I watch my dishes, one by one
tossed like toys in the river
while the fire eats the little furniture
I saved fifty years for;
my children
carry their children
like crosses on their back.
We walk many miles
through bombed-out villages
debris of people's homes
and all their worldly items.
We drag our weary bodies
across the Albanian border
where there are make-shift tents for sleep
and holes in the ground large as wounds
for us to defecate.

Eleanora's Collage

Her dead father
daring and handsome
drowns in the middle
of the other pictures.

He never saw
the blooming beauty of a daughter
at eighteen,
never heard
the symphonic crescendo
of her laugh,

but she sees him
seeing her
black and white tempura
dark eyes,
white shadows,
grey childhood
clouded by cancer,

tempting
the tattoo of memory
to discover color

in the cavities
of his eyes
of her eyes.

With Poems

    To Madge McKeithen, author, *Blue Peninsula*

Finally
a book—twenty years
in the making,
from the moment
he was a bud,
until now
broken boy
in a man's body.

Ill
without a diagnosis,
legs
no better than branches,
arms-
no leaves to wave with,

but a brain that burns
and a mother
who intravenously injects herself
with poems
to stay alive.

Other People's Laundry

    To Oseola McCarthy

For seventy-five years
she washed laundry-
dirty sheets,
grief,
knowing
certain stains are permanent.

Now
stooped-over
her arthritic joints
dance for joy,
since the $150,000 she saved
was given away
to a poor, black girl
like she once was,
so the young woman
can go to college
and wash her own sheets.

II. Mine

The Laundress

I'm a poet
different from others,
I do lots of laundry
spend hundreds
on Heavenly Clean detergent.
More than most poets,
I scrub and scour
persist
with grease and grime,
refuse to believe
in permanent stains.

I even wash
other people's
filthy laundry,
and enjoy
the caked vomit
of young children, the smelly semen
of lovers,
the sour sweat
of a night of sex and boozing;

I am willing to wash
all of this,

and if the bleach of my broiling labors
is insufficient,
laundress
that I am,
I'll get my hands wet
let the dirt destroy
these very puny nails,

again
again
again.

Vacation

Any day
the cabin-hutch might shut,
and I'll never
touch the wind
nor ride the waves again;

(I know the distance traveled
to grief;
I have journeyed there endlessly
including
in the heart of summer);

so I sail
every season cautiously
knowing today
when the sun is seductive
the wind rides free
my husband and children
are gloriously tan
and handsome,
that I can capsize
and any member of my crew
may go overboard.

One Shoe

My shoe flew
down
into the depths
of the subway
tracks,

while I walked
wobbly,
one foot clothed,
one bare,
my naked toes
touching
heated, harsh concrete

daring the sidewalk cracks
to dress me
in a different set of dreams,
defiant, perhaps
of the norms
I daily live,

when my feet
are buckled
and anchored.

Season of Sorrow

The season
I love
was dormant in my heart
for so long;
the flowers
fragrant with color
whose heartbeats
do a rumba
to the music
of the sun;
kept on dancing
while I first felt summer
when the sun
had lost its heart
and the day
went to sleep much earlier.

Amsterdam

I should have been twenty
when sex was in season
every minute;

I would have
delighted
in dining
at drug markets,
gazing
at the ripened, melon breasts,
bulging out of bras.

I could have indulged-
high on air or mushrooms-
my crying clitoris,

might have
walked away
from all of it,
but the store was open.

So was the body,
but now
here with my husband
weak with lusty libido,

I remind myself
I'm married
I'm a mother
I owe it to my children
who I tell,
"no Amsterdaming;"

to walk past
the Red Light District
past the Magic Mushroom Gallery
and Cannabis Museum;

to walk past all of this
follow the Anstel River
over the canals,
and gaze at the glorious sunsets
bleeding in the sky.

Grades

I grade your papers,
but there is no one
to grade mine,
I am left letterless
like an orphaned child—
no marks,
no comments
bland as a bark,

but when you look
beyond the hieroglyphics
my words bleed-
F,F,F.

Signals

Too many
stop signals;

listen,
I know
traffic rules,

but sometimes
the car
goes off course.

(Yes,
the driver should be
better prepared);

but sometimes
even an experienced road person
can tell you

signals get mixed-up
and I know you said stop,
I know you said red,

but I'm sick and tired
of your rules
and regulations,

as if
you're the only one
who can drive well;

like you're the traffic cop
who will decide
when you're off-duty.

Yom Kippur

In J.H.S.
we had played
simple games;
house, grown-up
putting on her mother's high heels
and lipstick,
sometimes we'd go shopping.

Today in temple
while praying
I spot her brother in the crowd;
he has grown tall and handsome
in the last twenty years.

"How's Susan?" I inquire.

"Schizophrenic
for the past ten years,
a vegetable,
she hardly leaves the house."

What kind, I wonder
a zucchini—tall, slender, remote
or maybe a potato
with eyes that gaze inward,
perhaps a tomato
her cheeks had been so red
and lovely.

The Tapestry

Grandpa
I'm knitting
your golden star
in my heart,
on this, the anniversary
of Babi Yar.

Knitting
is the barbed wire
that bound you,
is the sky you dreamed
when you wove wishes
not to leave
without being remembered,

for the words
you magically mixed
in the vials
that healed
the millions who lived
when they walked
into the temple
of your pharmacy,

not the millions
who died.

A Motherless Traveler

A geographic dyslexic,
Delaware
is up from New York,
Canada-
down;
west and east
perplex me,
even with a map
though eventually
I find my way.

With your body,
I'm completely lost,
there is no familiar river
I have swum,
no land
I ever lingered on,
nothing
to direct me,

but I recall
terrible terrain-
uneven rocks
loose-limbed branches
bruised and beaten,

I pined
for a path
that was clear.

So easy
to ride on, forever
never
return.

Longing

       To teenagehood

There was never the right wardrobe
clothes too big, too tight, too short,
or the right hair-
saturated with static
or thick-straight,
thighs as big as elephants
unkissed lips
filled with longing.

Sometimes I forget
when I'm hungry for the energy
to bounce out of my body
and pounce billions of beautiful bodies,

how bruised my body was, back then
except for when
someone else filled it.

The Journal

I never expected you, at seventeen,
to read my diary,
enter
unexplored territory
buried
at the bottom of the box.
Now you're wondering
sifting through layers
of leaves and words,
what happened to the woman
who wreaked havoc
in the wet snow
of wild, white pages-
lovers
and nude photographs,
lust spread thick like mulch
legs spread wide like the Grand Canyon.

What happened?
She became your mother,
the woman draped in an apron
dishing out your soup,
not the woman
you continue
to read.

Times Square, Christmas, 1960

Daddy
wasn't it wonderful
watching the world
 get dressed
for the holiday
while we performed
our special
day-in-the-city ritual;
you were always too busy
during the year,
but we had our day.

Wasn't it fabulous
gazing at the stars flash reds and greens
as cold
took a stab
at my face,
and crowds bounced off each other
like atoms.

Did you like watching
as much as I did,
or did it bother you
to always look
and never take center stage,

as you sit
perched in heaven's seat
knowing there'll never be
another entrance.

The Cape

I remember
the day I bought the cape,
and swirled like a dolphin
deliciously in the air;

I was happy
to wear a wardrobe
others had.
Fifteen and finally
normal.

The next day
friends
joined the parade of capes,
their rainbow of colors
flashing and flaunting,

while I
lamented the loss
of that moment
when I marched to their music,

but my stepmother
made me buy beige-
dull, pale,
able, like the earth

to sink lower
and lower
to hide beneath the cape
of the ground.

Death of an I.U.D.

It flooded out
like the infant
it had stopped
from being born.

It floated
in its pool of blood
fragile, tentative
lovely and little
as a lemon.

And now it's over-
the blood
the body
being birthed.

No more cycles
cycloning themselves
through my days
unpredictable and violent.

No more blood, period
like death
though I stand
breathing, eating, urinating
torrential rains.

There are still rains,
no storms
nothing unpredictable
for now,

before the older body
gets older,
the gates, narrower
and the bridge collapses
without a car
for no apparent reason.

Shroud Lifted

> To Ira, 29 years

Clean
as the star
stripped of gauze;

clean
as morning
before the wind
wakes up;

clean
as the infant's crib
cradled
in night's sleep;

clean
as deep-down detergent
caressing your cloth;

and your cloth
keeps me clean
and covered,

strips away
the shroud
of my once dirty heart.

In Harbor

      To Ira at fifty

I'll cross your ocean anytime
no matter the weather
whether it be a storm
so violent
the waves wage war
with water.

I'll weather the wild wind
the turbulent traumas of a hurricane
and of your undertow,

because I know
at the end of your journey
you dock
your shore is smooth as satin,

so safe
you anchor me
in harbor.

Sunset

"Come see the sun," I shout
watching it slip behind the clouds
like a thief,

but the son
is not interested.
At fifteen
he has better things to watch — breasts, bikinis,
barely-clothed girls;
this is why he came to Hawaii.

The green primordial fields
shimmering in volcanic cauldrons;
the ocean, gushing,
foaming at the mouth
rising erect as a stalk;
who cares about the scenery with the bodies
beautiful bodies.

The sun, now covered in total darkness,
but these bodies
set splendor in the sky.

Navigations

>   To Craig, 18

You are leaving —
your boat born of brittle wood
your sails like butterfly wings
could cross any ocean carefully,

only
if you don't pretend
that heavy-metals
and wrought-iron motors
are your composition.

There are many ways
to travel the sea
as long as you follow the compass
across the river
of your heart.

The Man

> To Craig, 21

To the boy
who was a baby
in my belly,

now a man
 marooned
on an ocean
without a sea,

there is a voice
deep within your ocean,

and it says,
"now you are free."

And it says,
"remember me."

Cruise Liner

    To Craig, 21

You've grown
into a cruise ship
whose restaurants
serve the richest meals-

and that's not all!
Your pools
are brimming with water,
your horn
bellows like a breeze of activity,
everyone wants a cabin,
an ocean view,

except for me
your mother
the small canoe
who watches you
forge out to sea.

Clean Laundry

      To Craig, 22

Washed
in the womb
of this machine,
hulking 6 foot 2 inch
boy-turned-man
on rinse & spin
so clean.

Metaphor

       To Samantha, 16

I asked the poet-
the sage,
who has published more volumes
than I,
but who also
has a schizophrenic mother
and writes about her
constantly,
does this-
the writing
settle the demons?
And she said, "no,"
they slither
like snakes in her sleep-
the words, the mother
swallow her
whole;

while I have found
in the folds of my flesh
a secret.

Sixteen years ago,
I birthed
a child
on the blank page
of my life,

and no metaphor
has ever measured meaning
made my mentally-ill mother
so obsolete
as this-

my daughter
the poem that has left my language
to grow its own rhythm
its own rhyme,
to invent a form
that has freed me of bad mother,
since I have written this poem
so perfect in the way
she's a new verse every day,

and I am the good mother
who created her voice,
her spirited, smiling
simile.

Departure

> To Samantha, 17

At the bottom
of this washing machine-
some lint, a penny
small, precious refuse
I refuse to rinse or spin,
gentle remains
of the little girl,
now wearing high-heels,
painted lips
Sartre in her back-pack.
She takes her laundry
with her.

Dry Cleaners

> To Samantha, high school graduation

Out of the cleaners,
your pressed smile
shows not one crease
of dissatisfaction;
the way you lay
perfectly folded on the couch,
form so beautiful
even off the hanger.
How to give shape
to such a wonderful wardrobe?

I did.
You did.
And now you're packed
and ready.

About the Author

Pamela L. Laskin is a lecturer in the English Department at The City College, where she directs The Poetry Outreach Center. Many of her poems, short stories and children's stories have been published in journals and magazines. World Audience Publishers recently published, *Ghosts, Goblins, Gods and Geodes*. *Secrets of Sheets* is Ms. Laskin's second book published by Plain View Press. Her first, *Remembering Fireflies*, came out in 2007. *Central Station*, her first collection of poetry, was the winner of the Millennium Poetry Prize, and three poetry chapbooks, two young adult novels and five picture books have been published as well. She edited *The Heroic Young Woman*, a collection of original fairy tales. She lives in Brooklyn, New York, with her husband, Ira. Her children, Craig and Samantha, are away at school, completing their degrees.

Pamela L. Laskin, 414 5th St., Brooklyn, NY 11215, 718-965-0746
bigapplepoetpam@aol.com

www.ingramcontent.com/pod-product-compliance
Lightning Source LLC
Chambersburg PA
CBHW071840290426
44109CB00017B/1882